Colleen,

Enjoy the journey of Gratitude.

All best,
Kelly Johnson

Gratitude

Cherry blossoms are the darlings of spring, a precursor to happiness. Their pink and white pillowy flowers are fascinating; they are well-mannered frenzies of pleasure. Softly they float above our heads, swirling about gracefully; when a petal falls and touches your face; it's like being kissed tenderly by an angel.

In my lifetime, I conveyed peace and joy, and I love flowers.

Copyright © 2022 Kelly Johnson Photography

All rights reserved. No part of this publication may be copied, displayed, extracted, reproduced, utilized, stored in a retrieval system or transmitted in any form or by any means, electronic, mechanical, or otherwise including but not limited to photocopying, recording, or scanning without the prior written permission of the author and publisher. If you would like permission to use material from the book (other than for review purposes), please contact kelly@photographykellyjohnson.com.

Thank you for being supportive of the author's rights.

Kelly Johnson Photography

2800 N Lombard Street # 144

Portland, Oregon 97217

photographykellyjohnson.com

Limited First Edition March 2022

ISBN 978-0-578-38095-7

Printed by Brown Printing Inc. Portland, Oregon. Thank you to their entire team.

Gratitude

Kelly Johnson

Photographs and Introduction by Kelly Johnson
Photographs Edited by Thiel Johnson

Publisher Kelly Johnson Photography · Portland, Oregon
Limited First Edition

Kelly Johnson PHOTOGRAPHY

"I believe in the true beauty of a flower. Keep it simple and honest."

Thiel Johnson

The choices you make today will chaperon your tomorrow.

Contents

Gratitude	1
The Blossoms	8
Afterword	76
About the Author	77
Acknowledgments	79
Appendix	80

When something ends, something extraordinary begins.

Gratitude

Springtime is gratitude. It is refreshing and new. The first sight of blue skies and flowers bloomin' sends my heart swoonin'. All my thoughts are of peace, beauty, and adventure when spring begins. It is a free-falling into majestic sublimity. The photographs in this book pay homage to my mother's teachings of gratitude, wisdom, joy, and love. Flowers, blue skies, and leaves represent those teachings. And it all happens in spring, hallelujah!

With all that has been going on in the world, I am grateful for another delightful spring. When I was growing up, my mother would say to me, "Have gratitude, Kelly." I did not know what she meant exactly. I felt as though I was grateful. My mother is caring; I had a roof over my head, food to eat, and clothes to wear. I was thankful for those things. My mother said that finding the meaning of gratitude would be life-changing. She was right. Today, my life has changed. Gratitude for me is finding peace and positivity in spring, and I embrace it with intention and verve. I practice gratitude every day, but spring is special to me. So, I focus on spring with my camera, graciously and gratefully.

My mother introduced me to gardening when I was ten. Looking over her garden, Mama's smile beamed like the sun and sparkled throughout our neighborhood. Her flower beds were magnificent: roses, pansies, violas, calla lilies, crookneck squash, cucumbers, and tomatoes. All flowers and vegetables flourished under her care and reflected her beautiful heart. A journey through her flower beds was a transition into simple splendor—her respect for the earth was unrelenting and precious. She taught me about soil, "the earth," she called it. "Our earth is rich," she said. "The texture is good, and its brown hue is striking and will bring us a great harvest."

If I close my eyes tightly, I can see my mother digging into the earth, planting seeds. I can hear her voice saying, "Kelly, please bring the water can. Isn't this fun!" It was my favorite time of the year to help with planting seeds. I felt vital, helpful, closer to my mother and the earth. Mama and horticulture went together seamlessly and joyfully. For her, gardening was life, renewal, growth, and brilliant possibilities. It also meant unity, hope, progression, and joy for the harvest and our family. It was so wonderful to see Mama, with her slender, five-foot six-inch figure, watering her garden while exuding serenity and humility.

Even now, every spring, I hear Mama's voice play sweetly in my head—a melodic tune. In Mama's day, her tone and texture were silk softly sidling along satin, refined and graceful. The grace of my mother was utterly charming and intoxicated those who were in her presence. Neighbors and children would stop by to talk to her about the weather or flowers. Mama's pleasantness drew people in, and her quiet elegance was captivating. Who would believe I would grow up to have a brown thumb after all my early training? I did not develop an aptitude for gardening, nor did my daughters. So, Mama would come over to my home every spring with flowers galore: petunias and violas piled high and peeking out of her car windows. Violas are some of her favorites. She would say, "They have cute, funny, angry faces: red, pink, yellow, symbolizing passion, health, and joy." I would get the gardening tools, and our floral journey of gratitude would begin. Mama and I would start digging into the soil; she would say, "People were happier and healthier when they were of the earth." Our happiness was unstoppable while planting, and our laughter was contagious. It was a utopia. I have learned flowers are dopamine, arousing our happy senses and making us feel delighted to be in their presence.

Flowers are boastful without voice. Calla lilies are full of attitude and stand tall, showing off their brilliant physiques—curvaceous lines and intermingled colors. Calla lilies leave me breathless, and then I surrender my heart to glorious beauty. Roses debut with extraordinary exquisiteness. They never disappoint; their petals are layered with lusciousness and excite us while caressing our senses. The popularity of roses is understandable; their delicateness and detail are notable. Although dahlias are not spring flowers, I included them. I would be remiss to exclude their exceptional beauty. The dahlias around the corner from my home are a fête. Their smooth, velvety petals are vivid, stunning. So stunning that after photographing them from every angle, I dive back into their meticulous and ambitious perfection and photograph them once again.

Blue skies, gray skies, and dogwood skies are remarkable. Dogwood flowers in my neighborhood are center stage, and it is swellegant. Pink ones and white ones tickle my soul. When the wind blows, they cluster and move as if they're at a big party dancin' a jig. Oh my goodness. It's a floral hootenanny! On quiet days, dogwoods are elegant ladies so soft and demure. Their grace is befitting their supreme gorgeousness—a cotillion that makes me smile and curtsy. They swoop me into heaven, and I rise in a cloud of joy.

Every spring, I fall in love with spring. The air smells of flowers bathed in sweet rainwater and seasoned with goodness. Vulnerability fills my heart, and humility hugs my soul. I must give flowers their due. They are little, feel-good beauties. They provide the world with fun, color, curiosity, and so much pleasure. Flowers are charming with a mystical power that stops me in my tracks and transcends me to euphoric heights. If I give them the time of day, they have me gushing and oohing and aahing all day long. Giddiness runs through my veins, and I cannot stop grinning.

To me, flowers and leaves are much like humans: they are tender, emotional, funny, full of swagger, demanding attention. "Look at me," they command, "watch me strut my stuff." A visit to the tulip field is full-tilt boogie, an exploration of diversity. The tulips' vibrant colors, shapes, sizes, and textures show that difference is fantastic. Imagine if all tulips were the same; a tulip field would be boring. Plunging into aromatic flowers is simply divine. The scents transport me to a time long gone. The bursting aroma leads me to recall memories of my grandmother's floral perfume and bliss-filled heart. Leaves brilliantly add depth and definition, complementing floral aesthetics. Leaves are determined, protective, and caring. They gather 'round flowers like a protective mother watching over her young. When the golden sun beats down on the flowers and leaves, they radiate hope. When a colossal rainstorm bathes them in dazzling crystalline raindrops, they sparkle and bling. When the wind blows its blustery breath, they sway with genuine joy and dignity. They thrill us. Whatever the weather, flowers, and leaves are lovely survivors.

I love watching admirers experience spring flowers; it is like watching an unveiling at a museum. Enthusiasts stare and smile and seem to take note of each color, the texture of petals, sunlight, and soil. When admirers watch me photographing flowers, they become involved in the process. With great inflection, they explain the origin, the intricate details, and the innate beauty of the flowers. I'm fascinated by their knowledge. Unfortunately, I don't know the names of most flowers. I always have to confess that I strictly photograph them for their enchanting beauty; my honesty immediately connects me with the admirers. I am shameless when I tell them I can't grow a thing. I share my gratitude with them about my mother, spring, and flowers and meeting people who adore them, about how grateful I am to photograph these little charmers.

Throwing an outdoor shindig for our daughters, my mother, and stepdad during springtime was awesome. The ambiance and the nuances of spring were essential for a successful dinner party. The table was always set, with bright tulips. Our neighbor's dogwood tree hung slightly into our yard and swayed with purpose as we bobbed our heads to sweet jazz. Our chats were of good cheer, renewal, and promise; the food was a feast of magnificent glory. Great emphasis on spring colors went into our culinary delights. I did the cooking, and my husband stylized the food plating. His platings blew everyone's mind: bacon-wrapped asparagus, mint leaves, and beets were tasty sprinkles of spring. Our blessings were abundant. As daylight dimmed, the embers from the firepit frolicked and crackled; my mother's enchanting smile casts a spell over all of us. It was an evening full of happiness and love inspired by spring.

My spring walks with my husband are a benevolent trek—the ideal melding of friendship and love. Spring is the backdrop to our love affair—an affair filled with passion, resiliency, imperfection, and beauty. It is also an opportunity for us to connect with God's glory: flowers, leaves, bees, dogs, and people. Spring is delicious and grand, and I adore it when my husband holds my hand. As we laugh and talk, we recall our thirty-eight years of marriage; we wink at each other and smile. I say to myself, "Spring, spring, you make my heart sing."

As spring whispers away, I'm brokenhearted. I want to shout, "Baby, come back!" as if we have broken up like lovers. As memories of spring sashay in my head, I am melancholy. Then I realize spring is for a season, a reason—time to refresh and renew; during spring, I flourish in my garden of new relationships and opportunities. For that, I am thankful.

Flowers are a staple in our home. Years ago, my mother said, "Kelly, let flowers rule the roost. Let them ripple throughout your home with grace and ease. They will add warmth and cheer; they are a pathway to conversations of joy and thoughtfulness." Tulips are my favorite; to me, their beauty is peerless. When they are paired together, they intertwine like sweethearts. They are pretty fascinating.

My mother taught me that gratitude is internal, that you have to look beneath the surface of life. One must look inward to find true beauty and contentment. When my mother and I were planting seeds, I learned we weren't just germinating flowers; we were growing a relationship—building a prosperous and unbreakable bond. I was the seed she planted, then a colorful blossom, and she was the loving nutrient stem. She promoted growth, provided energy, knowledge, and love, and watched me bloom. Her support for me was immeasurable; she immersed herself into motherhood with reverence and care. I am grateful she shared her life, wisdom, and love. My relationship with my mother will last all seasons—winter, spring, summer, and fall—a lifetime.

I am not without mistakes, but I did my best as a mother.
Mama, you raised the bar on motherhood and humanity.

The Blossoms

*Be careful with my heart;
I only have one heart to
love you with.*

Light is my guide—it moves through my soul with ease and elegance, and it is glorious.

Illumination is a passageway to health and tenderness.

Sometimes it takes courage to get out of bed. Get up and be courageous. Face the day and be grateful.

Ember leaves reaching for blue skies ignites the spirit and inspires the imagination.

Have a sense of adventure and discover new things.

Life will be your best teacher.

My parents were enthusiasts. My mother painted flowers, and my father was a photographer.

When the crowd stops roaring, be prepared to live your truth.

Disarm them with a smile.

I am different. I am abstract. I am beautiful.

Be the light in the room and shine brightly. Be better than the day before.

Blue skies will chase all your blues away.

*When I was sixteen,
I said to my mother,
"I will never work."*

*She said,
"Yes, you will.
Working Builds
Character."*

Take your shoes off and enjoy the walk.

Happiness is the pinnacle of well-being.

What is wealth?
Wealth is love.

All things are possible with love.

Bullying is not a strength; it is a weakness.

Love is strength.

You don't have to walk in someone else's boots to have empathy.

Intentional acts of meanness will only destroy you.

No is an opportunity. Failure is an opportunity. Forgiveness is an opportunity.

*Use your voice;
it is essential.*

*Twenty-five years ago, my mother gave me this yellow rose bush.
Every spring, she would come over and deadhead it for me. Amen, Glory.*

*My mother wore, Trésor. A rose fragrance, paired with earthy iris.
Trésor means treasure. So appropriate for my mother.*

*Success is a gift; I feel it in my soul.
It resounds with each breath I take.*

The subtlety of spring resonates with vibrancy.

Spring rain showers echo peace.

Sometimes stepping away from all of the chatter helps to hear more clearly.

Liberty, nothing can stop me now; I am free to learn, live, and love.

In 2020, the pandemic shut the world down. "People wanted to be heard."
Adults and children wrote messages of hope, goodwill, and warmth wherever and whenever possible.

A makeshift mural with words that became quite prevalent in 2020, "Black Lives Matter."

Yes, you are.

Where there is love, there is hope.

Diamonds and Pearls

One brisk spring morning, my husband and I were walking,
and it started to rain.

Rain fell from the sky and rested softly upon rose petals and leaves.

The raindrops glistened like diamonds and pearls, and it was breathtaking.

Raindrops are refreshing. They enrich the spirit and the earth.

*Raindrops celebrate renewal and hope, just like tears.
Give yourself permission to cry sometimes, and then rejoice.*

Leave your ego at the door.

Trust yourself to believe in yourself.

Gossiping is a reflection of you, not others.

Be a leader, not a follower.

Finding contentment is crucial and then victorious.

I am vulnerable. I am strong. I am love.

I'm Sorry. There is strength and character in an apology.

Accountability is splendid.

On our gratitude walk, we came across shadows of street signs that made the sign of a cross. Amen.

External beauty is transitory; internal beauty is endless.

A great leader is compassionate, diverse, and inspired.

Sing, dance, and be merry. Music and rhythm move the mind and body. Sometimes you just got to get your groove on.

The grass isn't always greener on the other side.
Sometimes you'll get to the other side, and you'll find out the grass is brown.

*Build a relationship with money. Respect your finances.
Pay your bills promptly and save appropriately.*

Celebrate your accomplishments.

People are Community.
People are supposed to be together to grow, learn cultures, and flourish.

You are the artist; design your destiny.

Witnessing vast splendor is seeing God's work.

*Life is beautiful, challenging, and fleeting.
Don't miss the journey.*

I shared my exquisiteness with all, and now, I will expire gracefully.

MAMA'S CUP AND FAVORITE BIBLE VERSE
"The LORD is my shepherd; I shall not want."
Psalm 23

Goodbyes can be sad, but they are necessary. They give us the strength to move forward, love, and accept the next part of our journey.

Afterword

To the readers, seek gratitude whenever and wherever you can.

My mother's love for gardening, spring, teaching, and family was the inspiration for *Gratitude*. My husband and I walked two miles a day during the spring pandemic of 2020. I photographed most of the flowers during that time; there are also beautiful hints of summer flowers throughout the book.

Positive moments in my life have made me smile and laugh and be kinder to others. Adverse moments in my life made me more forgiving and courageous, giving me purpose. Although my mother can no longer garden with me, I am grateful for our time together. Her wisdom has enriched my life. I am comfortable with who I am, and I am thankful. As much as my mother gave me, hopefully, I gave back to her.

My mother handed me some of her treasures throughout my adulthood. I often use her items in my work, it makes me feel as though time is standing still, that we are still chatting about life, love, and laughing brilliantly. In *Gratitude*, her bike, teacup, and the hats in the tulip field were highlighted.

My mother had many pithy expressions for life and love. She infused her kindness with common sense and love and shared it with me, with family, and with everyone she met. She often said, "Live in peace, Care for your fellow man, Forgiveness is necessary, and Hallelujah."

For me, having gratitude leads to happiness. Waking up is magnificent. Whatever the weather, I'm content. I don't take everything that happens personally. When I'm teaching life skills, I'm joyful. My friends are the best. Photography is a beautiful adventure, and loving my husband and daughters makes my heart beat with passion.

About the Author

Photos by Kelly Johnson

Nicole, Thiel, Kelly, and Natasha Johnson

Kelly Johnson is a nationally recognized photographer and children's book author, *Hair Dance (2007)* and *Look at the Baby (2002)* were published by Henry Holt & Company, New York. Hair Dance was one of The Best Children's Book of the Year 2008 selected by the Children's Book Committee Bank Street College of Education.

Johnson is also a nationally recognized fine art and notecard photographer. She is a certified life coach and a life skills teacher. Johnson spent her early years as a photographer for the Oregonian Newspaper Publishing Company. She has had ten photographic exhibits noted by the press. Johnson's photograph *Daddy's Shoes* is part of the Kresge Art Museum, Pacific Northwest Photographers Exhibition Permanent Collection, Michigan State University. Her work has also been published in magazines and newspapers.

Thiel Johnson is the photo editor of *Gratitude*. Johnson does not work in a creative field professionally, but his attention to creative detail is uncanny. He has an innate ability to edit photographs from a viewer's perspective. His thoughts of color, subject, and timing are fundamental. Thiel and Kelly Johnson have been married for thirty-eight years and have two wonderful grown daughters.

Kelly and Thiel Johnson

Gloria Ella Dean

Gloria Ella Dean is eighty-one years old. She is a loving mother of three children, a grandmother, aunt, and friend. Gloria is a retired business owner of Dean's Beauty Salon and Barber Shop in Northeast Portland, Oregon. Gloria's business is still flourishing, and in its sixty-seventh year—she understood her assignment: business owner, kindness, gardening, painting, wife, and motherhood. Gloria's mother, Rose Dean, called her daughter "Glory." Glory means triumph, beauty, and honor.

Acknowledgements

Gratitude is for my lovely mother,

Gloria Ella Dean, a brilliant mother and teacher

Love you, always

Thank you to my husband, Thiel Johnson, for the beautiful spring walks and talks

Love you, dearly

Thank you to our daughters, Natasha and Nicole

We love you both forever

Thank you to our neighbors and friends Lucille, Lily, and Nipsey

Love to all

Thank you to all the children in *Gratitude*

My mother, Gloria Ella Dean, and my father, William Marshall Brown, were instrumental in grooming my career as a professional photographer and a life skills teacher. I am so thankful.

Special thank you to the beautiful neighbors of Northeast Portland, Oregon, for sharing their flowers and gardens with us and my camera.

The tulip portraits were photographed at Wooden Shoe Tulip Farm, Woodburn, Oregon.

Thank you to Goran for his elegant book design for *Gratitude*.

Thank you to Eric Muhr for his editing guidance.

A portion of the proceeds from *Gratitude* will be donated to the Alzheimer's Association in honor of my mother, Gloria Ella Dean.

Photo by Nicole Rose

Kelly Johnson, daughter and Gloria Ella Dean, mother

Appendix

10 Light

11 Illumination

12 Courage

13 Ember Leaves

14 Adventure

15 Life

16 My Parents

17 Stops Roaring

18 Disarm

19 Beautiful

20 Shine

21 Blues

22 -23 Character

24 The Walk

25 Happiness

26 - 27 Wealth

28 Bullying

29 Love

30 -31 Empathy

32 Intentional

33 Opportunity

34 - 35 Your Voice

36 Every Spring

37 Trésor

38 – 39 Success

40 Subtlety and Vibrancy

41 Peace

42 Stepping Away

43 Liberty

44 Be Kind

45 Black Lives Matter

46 Yes

47 Hope

48 – 49 Diamonds and Pearls

50 Raindrops

51 Tears

52 Ego

53 Trust and Believe

54 Gossiping Reflection

55 Leader

56 Victorious

57 Vulnerable

58 I'm Sorry

59 Accountability

60 Amen

61 Transitory

62 - 63 Great Leader

64 Music

65 Greener

66 Money

67 Celebrate

68 People

69 Destiny

70 -71 God's Work

72 The Journey

73 Gracefully

74 Mama's Cup and Favorite Bible Verse

75 Goodbyes